World Class Software

A New Paradigm
for World Class Results

2ⁿᵈ Edition
Revised and Updated

By
Jonathan Cook

Visit the author's website for more information.

https://sites.google.com/site/jccookauthor/

Contents

Executive Summary

Let's face it—from a management perspective the only thing that matters is results. All the plans, processes and techniques in play matter little if they do not achieve results!

The software development process is no different. All that matters to management and the customer/client is a working product, delivered on-time and on-budget.

But frankly, this rarely occurs. Projects are constantly late and over budget. No matter what software development method is employed, the results seem to be the same: Poor!

Are your developers less productive and dispirited? Are your project managers constantly overloading your resources? Are bugs carried through to the final builds and into production?

The author provides this Executive Report to show you a different way to achieve quality results. It does not attempt to rewrite the existing tomes, but instead it offers new ideas, new ways of viewing existing processes, shines a light on the common issues and offers answers that you can adapt and incorporate into your software development process.

Introduction

In corporate management minds software development is widely considered to be an engineering discipline subject to standardized practices and factory floor techniques that can be applied to improve productivity, reduce bugs, improve performance, and in general make the entire development process smoother and easier, resulting in better outcomes.

Standardized disciplines such as Agile and Waterfall attempt to remove the variables from the development process with the goal of making software development much like an auto assembly line. The client request goes in at the start of the line and the completed perfect software system comes out at the end of the line in a predictable pathway of budgets, resources and time frames.

In the opinion of the author software development is NOT a process discipline. It is an art, a craft and a practice. It is emphasized in this and other Jonathan Cook Executive Reports that software development should not be seen as a factory floor solution, but as a creative solution. Art created on a factory assembly line may look like art, but it is a poor knock-off, at best, and a process nightmare at worst. What real artist wants to work on an assembly line? The human resource issues alone preclude the use of the pure process methods[1] as applied to software development.

So how do you satisfy the management need to deliver a product (let's face it, time, budgets and results are still important to the bottom line) with the art of software development? This Jonathan Cook Executive Report will guide you through a 30 day action plan to realign your team into the creative AND productive team it can and should be.

This report is neither a treatise nor a criticism on the Agile, Waterfall or other development models, but rather an analysis of the issues (as directly experienced/observed or researched by the author) surrounding them and a re-visioning of the best of all of them from a perspective of software as art and not as

---

[1]   The term 'methodology' is often mistakenly used as the term to describe the body of methods used to implement a process. As such, this report will use the term *model*. Some quotes and citations may use the term 'methodology(ies)'.

process.

This report draws upon decades of real-world corporate experience on projects worth many millions of dollars processing billions of dollars worth of money and information.

Jonathan Cook knows that you do not have time to read an encyclopedia of details so this report is short, concise and broken down into four 5-day work weeks of information gathering and concrete action plans that will transform your people into an effective development team while allowing them to work more effectively, hone their skills and love their craft (work).

A Quick Preview

Week One: Establish and create your model

    The Waterfall model

    The Agile model

    The author's perspective on software development.

    Establish your model

Week Two: Establish your teams

    What is a team?

    Agile teams

    Waterfall teams

    The author's recommended team

    The ditch digger analogy

    Assign and train fewer, smarter, local, non-contract resources

    Analysts

    Developers

    Quality Assurance (QA)

    Project Managers

    Trainers

    Support

    Management

    How should teams be formed?

    Who manages the team?

Dump the politics

Establish your teams

Week Three: Define your tools

Define your tools

Fewer, better tools

Management tools

Testing tools

Environments and Deployments

Support

Implement your tools

Week Four: Implement

Implement it all!

Change is hard

Expect issues

Make it fun

Point out the rewards

Encourage the craft

Two Days Left: Celebrate

Celebrate!

Week One: Establish and Create your Model

Common Models

This Executive Report is not designed to train you on the details and techniques of a particular software development model nor is it designed to criticize these models, but rather analyze key weaknesses. The strengths of these models are already documented by enumerable publications and consulting businesses. Instead, this report will review the basics of common models, show you key, but rarely documented, weaknesses, and then show you how to adapt them to work for your situation.

A software development methodology or system development methodology in software engineering is a framework that is used to structure, plan, and control the process of developing an information system. Common models include waterfall, prototyping, incremental development, spiral development, rapid application development, and extreme programming. A methodology can also include aspects of the development environment (i.e. IDEs), model-based development, computer aided software development, and the utilization of particular frameworks (i.e. programming libraries or other tools).[2]

The most common models most developers will encounter in the current corporate environment include Waterfall and Agile. Each can go under various names, but the overall theme is that Waterfall is a structured development process and Agile is an adaptive process.

---

[2] http://en.wikipedia.org/wiki/Software_development_methodology

Image courtesy of David Castillo Dominici/FreeDigitalPhotos.net

Waterfall

A common definition of the Waterfall model is:

The waterfall model is a sequential design process, often used in software development processes, in which progress is seen as flowing steadily downwards (like a waterfall) through the phases of Conception, Initiation, Analysis, Design, Construction, Testing, Production (Implementation), and Maintenance.[3]

Common weaknesses

Structured and Rigid

Waterfall is often considered to be too rigid and

---

[3] http://en.wikipedia.org/wiki/Waterfall_model

inflexible. The design must be followed at all costs until the customer requests a change or a design flaw is discovered. While this is generally considered a flaw in the process, it can also result in strengths if managed properly.

Little User/Customer Involvement

The customer is involved in the request and design process, but then has little contact with development and testing until the product is ready for delivery. This can allow the propagation of design flaws and bugs throughout the whole process, only to be discovered at the end when the problems are the most difficult to resolve.

However, the reality is that any development team, working with a customer of any significant size, will very likely run up against this issue regardless of the development process used. Unless your customer is deeply entrenched in the same development process that your team is using (and that process demands deep customer involvement), you will find that they are difficult to engage. This is one of the most difficult issues to resolve regardless of the development process used.

Documentation Overload

Waterfall is generally considered to be documentation heavy. There are customer request documents, preliminary designs, logical solutions, physical solutions, approvals and sign-offs, Quality Assurance contracts, etc., etc. This does not even include the myriad of developer documents involved with the design and

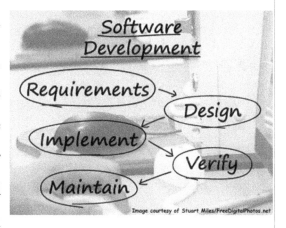

Image courtesy of Stuart Miles/FreeDigitalPhotos.net

commenting of the code. Teams can feel buried in documentation.

Flaws are Found Late in the Product Cycle

As mentioned above, design flaws and bugs can make their way though much of the product cycle before discovery. This often makes the resolution of these flaws and bugs very difficult.

Quality Assurance (QA) is Late to the Table

QA is often left out of the design and development process, only to be engaged and scheduled at the end of development. This makes the QA process difficult as they are unfamiliar with the product they are expected to test. Often bugs are reported that are not actually bugs, clogging up the process, or worse, bugs are missed.

Training and End-User Documentation are Late to the Table

Like QA involvement, customer training and end-user documentation are often after thoughts.

Project Scope Expansion

As a project evolves, it often picks up new customer requests that expand the scope of the original product. Rarely are features removed by customer request, only added. This obviously expands the work load and possibly the delivery times leading to project conflicts.

Project Drift

Similar to project scope expansion in its impact, project drift can cause a project to get off track. Drift usually occurs when project priorities are not clearly defined and development begins to spend too much time on less important features. Often, in Waterfall, all of the features appear to be of similar priority resulting in project drift.

Poor Code Review

One of the most often expressed criticisms of Waterfall is that there is not enough code review (formal or informal) to catch design flaws and bugs. Code review certainly has its benefits but frankly, from a customer perspective is often over rated.

Image courtesy of Adamr/FreeDigitalPhotos.net

Agile

A common definition of the Agile model is:

Agile software development is a group of software development methods based on iterative and incremental development, where requirements and solutions evolve through collaboration between self-organizing, cross-functional teams. It promotes adaptive planning, evolutionary development and delivery, a time-boxed iterative approach, and encourages rapid and flexible response to change. It is a conceptual framework that promotes foreseen interactions throughout the development cycle.[4]

Each model has its pros and cons. On paper, the Agile model appears to be the best and in practice Agile is being adopted by many development shops precisely because it does promise better results. However, promises and results can quite often be different.

Common weaknesses

Poor Documentation

One of the primary tenants of Agile is reduced documentation. Code should be self documenting (with few if any comments) and project documentation is held to a minimum. This generally results in poor communications, poor historical project knowledge and project confusion between the various elements of the overall team. Waterfall may have too much documentation but that is not an excuse to have too little documentation. This problem often relates directly to the other weakness listed in this section.

Poor Customer/Client Involvement

Ideally, domain knowledgeable customer representatives are part of the Agile development team,

---

[4] http://en.wikipedia.org/wiki/Agile_software_development

spending significant time side-by-side with the developers and QA representatives as the product is being developed. Business reality rarely allows this. The customers with the best domain knowledge are in great demand by many areas of the business and rarely have time to spend with the developers. Customers who may have time generally do not have the required domain knowledge. For large projects in large organizations this can be particularly difficult as many domains may need to be a part of the project.

The end result is poor customer involvement and relations. The author has observed a number of situations, in large organization, where the customer is not even aware that a project is in progress just when they are required to get involved in the development process. As such, development stalls and resources are left idle.

Poor Project Interface Management

In today's modern, large business projects a system is not developed in a vacuum. Rarely is a software system developed that just connects to a local database or presents a static web page. Large businesses interface with many different systems, each with its own interface requirements. This common situation almost always

conflicts with the ideals of Agile. Connecting to a local database may sound simple and easy to accomplish within an Agile sprint, but if the database team is not on-board with the Agile process, they may not meet the Sprint's goals or their design requirements may even conflict with the project design. Furthermore, necessary Web Services may not exist and Security departments may refuse network access or impose cumbersome connection requirements.

The common solution is to mock the various interfaces such that the rest of development can proceed. This works for a short time, but there comes a point when the real interface is required. In addition, the mock interface rarely accounts for all of the nuances of the real interface.

Poor Time Management

Agile promises that team members, overworked by other development processes, will now work in an environment free from extraneous distractions with clearly defined goals contained in well defined time sprints. The work will be less stressful and more sustainable.

The author has yet to observe this. The common reality of business is such that developers are often pulled aside to attend to issues of legacy software, other projects running in parallel with the primary project and a myriad of HR and other non-project related tasks. Just recording project metrics, as often demanded by management, can result in significant loss of productive time.

In addition, project managers, intent on making sure their project plans look good, rarely buffer for vacation and sick time off. Many can't even properly resource an FTE (Full Time Equivalent) resource.

Poor Quality Assurance (QA) Involvement

This is similar to poor customer/client involvement. Good QA practices state that the people testing a system should not be the same people developing the system (similar to Separation of Duties in Generally Accepted Accounting Principals). As such, the QA team has to schedule their involvement with the Agile practice much the same way as the customer. This can result in similar problems.

Image courtesy of Renjith Krishnan/FreeDigitalPhotos.net

Pairing is Counterproductive

Developer pairing is one of the primary goals of Agile. Pairing is designed to encourage ongoing code reviews; faster, more productive coding sessions (cleaner code through continuous re-factoring); cross training of the developers (as stronger developers naturally teach weaker developers); and training to the larger code set, as the developers are exposed to more of the project code.

Unfortunately, the author has not observed these results in real practice. The reality of pairing often results in:

Personality Conflicts: These include the typical interpersonal issues that strongly creative people face when working close together (artists often do not work well together) and stronger developers are hindered and annoyed by weaker developers.

Resources are Idle: Even with the proper tools, only one person can type code at a time. This leaves one developer idle. This may be the stated goal of Agile as the idle developer can observe the working developer and catch any errors. See personality conflicts.

Remote Issues: In today's world developers are often remotely located and work over the wire. This can create additional issues such as poor communications, keyboard conflicts, internet/network outages, etc.

If the business customer/client resource and QA resource are not also remotely available then the developer pair may end up idle.

Pair Schedule Conflicts: This may be as simple as bathroom and lunch breaks to as complex as vacation and other time-off conflicts. Agile states that any one person can pair with any other person at any time, but this rarely works well in practice per the other listed issues. In addition, people naturally work at different paces and conflicting paces will stress one and bore another.

A Few Good Developers End Up Doing all of the Work: This is particularly vexing as strong developers tend to do the bulk of the work. Ideally, the weak developers will become strong developers, but as is often the case the strong developers just dominate and the weak developers get frustrated.

Lack of Privacy: Working in pairs in a large development room leaves little privacy and private space. Humans are naturally social, but also naturally private. Both of these are stressed when people are *forced* into group (and pairing) situations.

Lack of Ownership and Responsibility: Agile states that developers should not own their code and that everyone is responsible for all of the code. This sounds ideal, but much like socialism it often results in no-one taking responsibility for code and bug fixes.

Teams are too Big and Hard to Manage

Agile teams can be large or small depending on available resources and team design, however they are generally a minimum of four to six people. A project may consist of several teams and these may cross-matrix with multiple other teams from other departments which may in turn matrix with other departments. A spider web of interaction can occur which creates management conflicts (project and personnel).

This can be a problem with any development model, but Agile's loosely coupled, self-organizing, cross-functional team model can aggravate standard management practices as the process will likely conflict with org charts and established authority pathways.

Sprints are too Short/too much Work

This is similar to poor time management but is directly related to Sprint duration. Sprints must allow for all of the elements required.

Project Scope Expansion

This is essentially the same scope issue found in other development models. However, Agile's loosely coupled, self-organizing, cross-functional team model can aggravate this as different teams accept new scope

Image courtesy of Stuart Miles/FreeDigitalPhotos.net

requests independent of other teams and without a central coordination process.

Incomplete Projects

Agile's goal is to balance Scope, Resources and Time. A lack of resources means that scope must be reduced or time extended. Similarly, a lack of time means more resources and/or less scope. This equation can play out in multiple ways such that the balance results in an incomplete project.

Ideally, if all parties agree to all balancing of the equation then an acceptable (though not necessarily ideal) project outcome is the result.

Business Reality Rarely Cooperates

Rarely can business just expand resources and/or time. As such, scope is usually adjusted resulting in a poor skeleton of the original project. Multiple releases of the project then follow and eventually a real product emerges. However, with all of the other issues listed, the entire process may result in a miserable project experience and little enthusiasm for the next project (or more likely the same project's new releases still developing in parallel).

Focus Evolves to the Code Quality Rather than to the Results

Early in this report it is strongly stated, whether we like it or not, that all that really matters is a working product, delivered on-time and on-budget. However, Agile's strong emphasis on code quality and re-factoring tends to encourage the team to focus more on the nuances of code quality then on actual results. From an artistic and craft perspective this sounds ideal, but from a business perspective it can hinder progress and result in poor outcomes. Business cares only that code WORKS and solves the problem at hand. It does not care how nuanced the code is. Code should not be flawed from a functional perspective, but it does not need to be perfect from an artistic or engineering perspective.

Many would argue that high quality, self-documenting code allows for better code maintenance and enhancements. Rarely is this actually realized in the real world. Any code later reviewed and modified by the original developer will already be understood by that developer (although very old code is often forgotten even by the original developer) and a new developer will have to mentally reverse-engineer even the best of code. This is further aggravated by Agile's insistence on reduced documentation and code comments.

The Author's Perspective on Software Development

As previously emphasized, software development is NOT a process discipline. It is an art, a craft and a practice. It is emphasized in this and other Jonathan Cook Executive Reports that software development should not be seen as a factory floor solution, but as a creative solution.

As such, none of the current software development models truly satisfies this reality. One can argue that Agile best fits this reality but in common practice this is not true. In fact, Waterfall even with its structured design, can often better satisfy the software as art paradigm.

The author's decades of experience has taught that in order to drive quality outcomes and produce excellent results, the developer resources must be thought of as artists and not as bodies. Developers are not just organization chart entries. They must be seen as creative assets rather than numbers.

This may seem like an obvious conclusion and one that has been touted in management journals for decades. However, when rubber-meets-the-road and metrics do not align with goals, often the first hatchet blows fall upon the heads of the very people that are the solution, not the problem.

For example, how many times has a project fallen behind in the schedule and the first response is to drive the developers (and other people) into overdrive, demanding more work in less time, cutting vacations, working overtime, etc.? Does this work? It may produce some results for a short time, but constant pressure of this type will actually reduce results.

Or— new resources are hired and added to the teams with the expectation that more people will produce more results. This also tends to fail to produce the expected outcome if for no other reason then the current resources are pulled from real work in order to bring the new hires up to speed with the project. It can take months for a new resource to be truly effective in a new environment.

As you will see below, there are better solutions.

The Developer as Artist and Development as a Craft.

It has been emphasized multiple times in this report that the developer is an artists and not just a technical resource. Of course there are many arguments against considering developers as artists and the author does not take the perspective that software is only art or that the

Image courtesy of Adamr/FreeDigitalPhotos.net

developer is only an artist. Frankly, most business solutions make rather boring art displays and pure artists are often undisciplined nuts.

And many would argue that because software development is technical in nature, it must be science and engineering, not art. Thus, only strict process and organization can produce good results.

The truth lies somewhere in between and each business environment will have its own nuances that make it a unique environment. Only you can know the exact environment in which you work and/or manage. You need to make the final decisions on implementing your model and process.

Given that, The author takes the perspective that software development is an art and a craft. The artistic perspective states that it is a creative process that requires imagination converted into results. The craft perspective states that it can be defined within a process that actually does convert the imagination into results. Both work together to take an idea (requirement) and convert it into a result (solution).

There are, of course, many articles and books on how to translate the creative process into real solutions (in any field). However, for the software development process there are a number of concrete elements and steps, rarely addressed, that will be covered in this report. More on this to follow, but quickly, they include:

Clearly define your team and the individual's roles: In the real world individuals (and especially software developers) are pressed to do more for less. This can be counterproductive.

Let your team members be experts in their fields: You will get better results from experts than generalists.

More resources (developers) do not translate to better results.

Retain your talent: Make them want to stay with your organization.

Promote and promote from within.

When you do recruit, hire local talent: They will be more dedicated.

Hire resources proficient in the language of your site and business: If your site works in English be sure everyone speaks English well.

Do not use short term contractors.

Interview recruits in person: At the very least do this at the end of the interview process. Many a recruit has sounded wonderfully competent on the phone simply because they Googled the answers during the phone interview.

Do not hire out of schedule desperation: Give yourself time to find the right people. Then KEEP them.

Establish your Model

The challenge then becomes applying the Artist and Craft perspective to the development model that is already in use in your environment or to the model that you will choose to implement (if a new one at all!). This may sound difficult, but it is more a matter of re-visioning and applying attitude and subtle actions to the model than the wholesale re-working of the model.

Week One Action Plan

Decide to View Software Development as Art and Craft Rather than Factory Floor Assembly Line

This is a critical action item! If you are convinced that software development is purely a process of science and engineering, and developers are seen only as tools to be managed, then stop here and save yourself the time of reading the rest of this report. Otherwise please continue.

Select your Development Model (or validate your existing model)

This will take more research than presented in this report. If you already have a model in place then you have already done your research. Is it working? Can it be improved? If you do not have a model in place then you can begin your research using the details and references in this and other Jonathan Cook Executive Reports.

Review the Other Jonathan Cook Executive Reports

A number of these will apply to the long term success of your model and team.

If Required, Take your Plans to the Next Management Level for Approval

This action item is, from the author's perspective, an optional action item. Many of the action items in the following sections can be implemented at a team level without undo impact to other teams with which your team may interact. While no team works in a vacuum and every change can have impacts to the interfaces with other teams (of which you may have no control or influence), most of the action items the author recommends are designed to be team internal and not corporate structural in nature.

With that said, the final decision is yours to make. If you are making wholesale changes such as implementing a whole new model, then this may impact the communication dynamic of the team and it will thus have broader cross-team or even HR implications. In addition, some models (Agile in particular) require significant levels of additional client interactions and even integration with teams, further complicating your plans.

Week Two: Establish Your Teams

What is a Team

A simple definition of a team might be a group of people who come together to achieve a common goal or outcome.

However, in the corporate world a team can be more complex. The corporate world imposes restrictions (budgets, org charts, HR rules, etc.), boundaries (internal Do and Don't rules, department structures) as well as lack of structure (cross matrix teams often result in conflicting loyalties and reporting hierarchies).

As such, in the corporate world a team might best be defined as a loosely coupled collection of resources than can *effectively* accomplish a goal.

Effectively is a key word. Teams can be organized from a collection of resources, but if they are not effective then they are essentially worthless and should not be a team.

To form an effective team you must know both what goal you want to achieve as well as the resource requirements to achieve the goal. This is not always simple.

From a software development perspective, the goal is usually spelled out in some type of requirements

Image courtesy of Renjith Krishnan/FreeDigitalPhotos.net

document. This often comes from a team that is originally separate from the actual development team that will implement the requirements. Later the requirements team will likely work with development teams on the project.

The resources (and we are considering HR resources to make up the team) are made up of the expertise required to implement the goal. This may sound obvious, but is often the most perplexing part of the process.

An Example

Let's describe a real scenario experienced and resolved by a resource known to the author. Although this example is not strictly a software development scenario, the team principals and dynamics still offer important lessons.

> *This example occurred in a large organization some years ago. In this organization it was decided by a new management team that all organization change should now be determined and implemented by self organizing, cross functional staff level teams. These teams would spot problems in the organization, develop solutions and, depending on the size and complexity of the solution, implement the solution. Large solutions required a higher level of management interaction.*

> *In theory, this new design would let the staff determine and define the issues and solutions,*

empowering them to take control of their jobs, work environments and careers. Upper management would then be free to deal with the enterprise level concerns.

Early on a majority of the staff felt positive about the new design and the theoretical benefits that it promised. Teams were organized with volunteer members eager to take on the self-management tasks with the hope that addressing known problems and implementing self-management would remove much of the drudgery of the typical staff level position.

However, the results were far from promising. The self organizing teams that developed were generally composed of two types of people: Weak performers who just saw the management meetings as a way to get out of real work, and management wannabes looking for something to manage. The productive staff were the artists of the work force and just wanted to do the job they enjoyed and found rewarding. To the artists the new teams were seen as unproductive side shows designed to placate the masses.

By the time that the new staff resource (known to the author) took over the leadership of one of the teams (at the request of upper management) the self organizing teams had devolved to department party and event planners. At the recommendation of the new resource the team was dissolved by upper management. A short time later all of the self organizing teams were reviewed and dissolved and not long after that the upper management responsible for implementing the teams was removed and/or reorganized by the board.

An Example: Lessons Learned

Self organizing, collaborative teams look promising in theory, and certainly can result in good outcomes under the right conditions. However, theory does not always result in planned outcomes. In this example management assumed that people wanted more control and would take the initiative to identify and solve the issues at hand. The results were far different.

There was little if any prioritization of identified issues: Small issues received as much attention as large issues, maybe even more depending on the staff hierarchy of who complained the loudest.

Team leadership was weak at best, non-existent at worst.

No additional pay was provided and no time was allotted from staff work schedules to participate in the teams resulting in volunteer teams that devolved into mere social gatherings.

The teams had no real authority: Even if a team reached a solution, it rarely had the authority to implement it. Budgets and resources were still controlled by upper management, and teams had no structural authority over any staff. As such, solutions were rarely implemented.

Upper management never got involved with the teams and there was no leadership or support. Teams eventually realized that upper management was merely tossing them the proverbial bone. The teams eventually self organized into event planners.

The artists did not get involved*:* They were doing the real work.

Dissolve the team when it is no longer effective!

Unfortunately, at this point in time, the author has yet to see a truly effective self-organizing, collaborative team that theory suggests. But hope is not lost...

Agile Teams

Agile teams come in all shapes and sizes depending on the flavor of Agile that is implemented. It is important to note that Agile heavily emphasizes the team concept in such a way that it is easy for a business to consider the team as more significant than the project itself. Agile states that teams should be *collaborative, self-organizing* and *cross-functional.* While this sounds wonderful, in practice real definitions and practical implementations for these team attributes are few and rarely successful in the ideal form.

Waterfall Teams

Teams in Waterfall are generally much more structured and management driven. Management, along with project managers, review resource requirements and then organize teams appropriate to achieving the goals.

Again, theory supports that this should work effectively as management knows its resource capabilities and is in control of their allocation. However, theory often hits the real world head on as competing organizational needs stretch or misallocate resources and project managers misjudge project time lines and (usually) significantly under allocate resources.

The author recommends a new way to look at teams.

Teams cannot be completely free to self-organize as artists tend to be too independent. However, your resources are experts in their field (or don't hire them) and can certainly collaborate on a project. As such, the team needs to be organized using a happy medium of independence and management guidance.

Project specifications should drive the resource needs of the team. Waterfall projects tend to have more involved specifications than Agile projects. Regardless, it is recommended that both models have some type of formal written specifications. Formal written specifications are the driver for resource planning.

Once a project is selected for development the department members (usually a superset of the eventual project development team) should quickly meet to hash out high level resource requirements. Since your resources are experts, this should take little more than half an hour. You are looking for high level input. For example—will the project involve database resources, mid-tier development, client development, what languages, etc.

These types of questions will define the expertise required and thus the general resources and tools required. You can quickly allocate a requirements spec review team to further refine the resources required for the project.

Caution: Do NOT assume that your expert resources have the time to take on even this early level of effort for a new project! Be sure to allocate the time required in relation to other on-going efforts. Consult with your project manager(s) and the expert resources to make this determination. Assume that they will not have time and be cautious even if they tell you they have time. Artists as expert resources will almost always want to discover the next project and please the boss. It is in their nature as artists to *display* their work and work effort.

Fewer smarter people

Many organizations, managers and the project managers have a tendency to push for more resources in the mistaken believe that more resources will complete a project faster and better than fewer resources. Resources should be allocated to the actual requirements of the project and not to either the available resources (which may be plenty in a large organization) or a perceived tight time line.

This may sound counter intuitive, but in the development paradigm of developer as artist and process as craft, a smaller number of artist developers can often achieve more and better quality work than a larger team of engineer developers.

When a project plan takes on the purely mathematical model of balancing resources, time and scope it is almost always doomed to at least significant problems if not outright failure.

Time is relatively easy to review as a project moves along. You either have a deadline or not (let's assume you always have a deadline). You either meet the deadline or you allocate more time (as painful as that may be in the real world). You cannot create new time, slow it down or speed it up.

Scope can be variable and in the Agile model it is expected that scope is variable. Working with your stakeholder you adjust scope to meet the time and resource requirements. In theory this works, but in reality stakeholders are disappointed, the project may be so incomplete as to be worthless, and without admitting it, the displaced scope is simply added to another *Phase Two* project time line and the end result is simply to add time to the project.

As such, the most common adjustment is to the resources. However, this is more often than not, an utterly misunderstood adjustment. Much like Pavlov's dog, project planners are conditioned to add resources in the generally false believe that it will speed up a project.

The ditch digger analogy illustrates this well.

The Ditch Digger Analogy

Consider the process of manually digging a 100 yard ditch (for now, ignore how deep/wide it is or that it could probably be completed with a machine). It will take one ditch digger one day to dig one yard of the ditch. Thus one ditch digger can complete the ditch in 100 days. The project planner mathematically assumes that five diggers can complete the ditch in 20 days and ten diggers can complete it in 10 days. Well, if that is the case then 100 diggers can complete it in one day and 200 diggers can complete it by lunch!

However, what the project planner fails to realize is the diminishing returns of too many ditch diggers. At some point there will be so many ditch diggers that they will beat themselves silly with so many swinging shovels and so much flying dirt. The diggers get in the way of each other and slow down the progress of the ditch. It is an art, combined with logic that can best determine the optimum number of ditch diggers.

Such is the art and logic of planning a software development project. You just cannot add more resources and expect mathematically increased project progress. There will be too many hypothetical diggers, shovels and loads of dirt. This is generally represented in cross-training efforts and bug fixes imposed on the experienced developers as they try and bring new resources up to speed on the project. You actually slow down the progress of a project rather than speed it up (this also applies to projects in which even experienced resources are continually shifted from one project task to another).

The author recommends that you assign and train to a

project fewer, smarter, local, non-contract resources rather than simply more resources.

Fewer Resources

This is important as described in the ditch digger analogy. You do not want them stepping on each other or standing idle waiting for work. In addition, fewer resources allows your team to become experts in the project subject matter as well as the tools used to build the project. When a resource is truly working at full capacity on a project they should be able to work in such a way as to rarely consult a technical manual, and rarely require a spec review. In other words, they are fully tuned into the project and can work at full speed.

A resource in this mode is not only more effective for the project, but they are more satisfied with the work they are doing. They know what they are doing, make good progress, (should) receive proper encouragement and reward and, most importantly, know exactly what to do when a bug/issue is found.

A developer as artist sees code not as words, but as a type of music. Much as a musician sees the sheet of music as a whole, and not just as individual notes, a developer with intimate knowledge of a code set will see it as a whole, moving through it much like a musician moves through music. This is not to say that a developer does not read and edit the code as individual lines and elements, rather it means that the experienced developer/artist can move through code in a rapid, fluid pace and make changes efficiently and with fewer errors, knowing better the interrelationships of the entire code set.

Smarter resources

This does not mean higher I.Q., but rather higher domain and subject experience as well as good interpersonal, language and writing skills. Assign to the project those resources that understand the business and project subject domain the best and can communicate the best.

This is obvious in casual reading, but often overlooked in the real world. Management will often assign a resource based only on availability and/or a single technical skill while overlooking the business and subject domain experience.

Business and subject domain experience brings to the

table more than technical skills. It weds the very important technical and domain interrelations that are often overlooked by purely technical knowledge. In other words, when developing a project there is more than just the technical elements, there is the understanding of how a system interacts with the business as a whole. Does the product need to send and/or receive data from other business components? If so, in what formats and through what channels? Who are the authorities that control those channels and what process is required to access those channels and get the project rolling with the least resistance from other teams. An experienced resource with good domain knowledge can cut through these issues with the best efficiency.

Local resources

Local does not mean in the same town or office as resources can be efficient regardless of physical location (albeit time zone differences can create some difficulties). As such, this is misunderstood in today's management paradigm (in addition, the politically correct push for diversity can directly impact this recommendation). Instead, local means cultural and language local. For a team to be at peak effectiveness it should not have to deal with language and cultural barriers. And simply working in the same language does not necessarily mean that everyone understands the same words in the same way. Accents and the cultural use of words can create difficulties in expressing and understanding thoughts and meanings. The author has seen this create major impacts and delays to projects. As such, the common language should be a localized version as much as possible.

In addition, The author has seen language and cultural barriers create interpersonal misunderstandings such that one persons compliment is another's insult. One persons innocent curiosity is another's horrid affront. This can create significant barriers to a team as once these lines are crossed, good relations are hard to recover.

This has nothing to do with nationality, race, religion, etc. It has to do with language skills and cultural experience. Anybody can have these skill sets. It is up to you to hire those that do.

Non-Contract Resources

There is a big temptation in management to hire temporary workers in today's global economic times. The author recommends that you do not hire temporary workers. Instead hire fewer full time workers per the previous reasoning.

The author has met, interviewed and worked with a wide variety of contract resources and these temporary workers can meet the recommended attributes as already discussed. However, on average you will have to weed through more candidates in order to find the few that meet the recommended attributes and, more importantly, you will likely lose these contracted resources at just about the time that they become fully effective with both the required business and technical domain knowledge in your projects.

In theory you can hire the contract resources at the end of their contract, but this can be problematic in larger organizations with less flexible HR rules, and done improperly you can run afoul of the IRS. In addition, contract resources are already familiar with changing jobs and locations and are often more than willing to leave your organization for the next one. In fact, some are in their contracting role specifically for the opportunity to travel to, and work in, a variety of locations.

Contract resources tend to be less vested in your organization and project as they know from the beginning that they are temporary. This is not to say that your full time hires are going to be perfect, but your chances are better.

On paper, contract resources can appear to be less expensive then permanent resources but generally, in the long run, the cost of continually replacing resources as their contracts expire (and losing the investment in training, business and project domain knowledge) is more than the cost of the permanent resource.

Another factor to consider is that the contractor may take valuable inside information to a competitor.

Plan to Train
In today's world management expects that every IT resource knows everything from the first day. Resumes are regularly padded with every acronym and keyword in the industry in hopes of triggering interviews from head-hunter search engines. The author has yet to meet anyone who really knows everything listed on their resumes. At best they have been exposed to the items and are expert in a few key items, at worst they Google these items

during the phone interviews in order to sound good to the interviewer (the author has experienced this not-so-subtle technique multiple times).

As such, plan to allow the resources you do hire the time to train on any tools and techniques needed to meet the project requirements. Do not assume that your resources know everything. However, if you have good resources, they can learn rapidly and on their own, given the time.

It is not always necessary to train in a formal classroom setting. In fact this can often be less effective to the artist developer that learns more from curiosity and exploration. Each situation and resource can be different so try and adapt as needed.

Analysts, Developers, Quality Assurance (QA), Project Managers, Trainers, Support, Management

This section will not describe the roles of the team members as this is generally well understood. However, there are unique attributes to these roles that are often overlooked or poorly used in today's organizations.

Each of the development methods in use in today's organizations utilizes some variation of the listed roles and their interrelationships. Much of this has already been discussed here or in other literature. As such, this section will highlight these overlooked elements of each of these roles.

Analysts (often referred to as a Subject Matter Expert (SME) or Systems Analyst)

A good analyst has a broad domain knowledge in some or all of the project (depending on the project size) and good relations with the business and management teams. They can be a good resource between the client, the developers and the rest of the team. However, analysts are often used only to create the initial specs, and maybe a few other project definitions, than they are sent off to work on another project, drawn back to the original project only when there is a misunderstanding (and often too late).

While analysts are generally not managers, they can be good coordinators. One key role often overlooked is their ability to see the big picture that encompasses the project design and the developer's tasks. Regardless of the development method employed, a developer will only work on a small snippet of the project at any one time. The analyst is in the best position to see how this fits into the overall project. Most importantly the analyst can feed the developer critical design elements that allow the developer to focus on implementing the design element rather than attempting to see the whole project as the analyst does.

For example, one of the best project development processes the author has seen was utilized such that the developers created a middleware code model of highly repeatable module design patterns (not reusable as each module performed different tasks) working through standardized interfaces to all other elements connected to the middleware. We will call this the Widgets project.

In the Widgets project all design elements passed data via the method signatures defined in the interfaces. Each method had one or more (overloaded) signatures defined such that all inputs and (returned) outputs to/from the middleware were well defined (this may sound obvious, but is actually rarely implemented in a planned, structured, repeatable fashion).

The Widgets project took advantage of the analysts knowledge of the whole project such that the analyst pre-defined the methods and their signatures because the analyst knew, from a high level, the data that needed to move back and forth for each of the required processes of the project. The analyst did not code, but rather defined the interface. The developer could then use the highly repeatable module design pattern to code to the requirements of the method signature. The developer did not need to understand the whole project, only the method signatures provided.

All aspects of the Widgets project worked

this way such that developers only coded to the interfaces in and out of their modules. The database experts followed the same routine focusing on their knowledge domain as did the client developers.

It was not unusual for significant new functionality to be defined, coded and integrated into the Widgets project development build in a matter of minutes or hours rather than days. Few bugs occurred and the project was completed before the deadline and under budget. Business was fully satisfied with the results and the system eventually went nationwide for that organization.

The Widgets project required one analyst, two (force paired) client developer, two (force paired) middleware developers and one database developer. Eventually it was realized that the paired client and middleware teams were less effective working as pairs than as individuals. The pairs broke up and *development accelerated.*

Developers

Much of this report has focused on the developers of a project. Noted here are the overlooked roles of a developer that have more to do with what a developer is NOT rather than what is a developer.

A developer is not a trainer. A developer is not a tester (QA). A developer is not a project manager or a general manager. A developer may be a lead developer, but unless that lead developer is specifically given domain HR authority, do not ask the developer to manage people in an HR capacity.

Above all, a developer is not a primary support person! If you want a developer then let the developer develop!

Of course, every business is different in size and requirements. The members of a small team may naturally have to take on multiple roles in order to complete a project. However, each team resource should know their primary role and their primary responsibility and be assured that they can focus on the primary and not be overly distracted by the secondary (or tertiary, etc.).

A developer must be allowed to focus. It is well known amongst developers that a single quick phone call interruption can kill 20 minutes of effective development. An experienced developer who is focused can produce code rapidly and with few if any errors.

Developers are not QA level testers. There are a number of titles and labels for the various testing schemes at the various levels of development but developers generally perform unit tests on their code.

Unit tests are fine but a number of development methods stress unit tests to the point that they should take up as much as half of the coding effort. The author takes the perspective that unit tests are appropriate for discrete modules that have testable components. However, not all parts of a project are easily unit tested with automated tools and spending too much time developing unit tests can be counter productive.

It is a better use of resources to develop manual routines to test the code (arguably these could be considered manual unit tests). You can review http://en.wikipedia.org/wiki/Unit_testing for more details.

Quality Assurance (QA)

The QA team is generally the final authority on the quality of the project prior to release to the customer (the customer is always the final authority).

QA resources should be thought of much like valuable developers. Not doing so results in inexperienced and frustrated QA resources that tend to move between projects (or worse, jobs) and constantly need new training on the systems they are testing. Under these circumstances they actually delay the development process rather than improve it.

Regardless of the development method used, the QA team should be involved from the beginning of the project. They can begin developing testing scenarios from the requirements and, working with the developers and analysts, adjust these as the project progresses. Some development methods insist that the QA person sit alongside the developers and client as code is developed. The author has not seen that as a particularly effective use of the QA resource. It is better that QA consult with the team as needed.

The QA team may have tools to test software, but much of the process is still manual and time should be generously allotted to testing.

There is some controversy as to the tools and techniques required to report bugs back to the developers. Some development methods insist that developers do not own the code and that anyone can work on anything. This often results in the QA team reporting bugs in a central database ordered by priority. In theory, the highest level bug is addressed by the first available developer.

In practice the author has not seen this technique work effectively. Without ownership there is a tendency to not take responsibility. In addition, if the bug is unfamiliar to the developer in line to take on the bug fix, the time required to determine the issue and fix it is often far longer than for a developer who knows exactly what the bug report means.

However, the QA team may not know to what developer the bug should be assigned. Or the QA team may assign it to the wrong developer and that developer must spend time reviewing it and reassigning it to the proper developer.

Good personal communication with QA and developers as artists and development as craft will naturally address some of these vexing issue. QA will know better to whom to assign a bug and developers, out of personal pride, will take ownership and will attack a bug as soon as they identify it in the QA report.

Project Managers

There is an entire industry surrounding the project management profession. The author has yet to see an effective project manager.

The main problem the author has found with project management for software development is too little focus on resource loading, and too much focus on time lines and task definitions. Put bluntly, all of this is due to the common fact that project managers are clueless as to software development. Even if a project manager is a former developer, chances are their lead project manager (driving the staff project managers) is clueless.

The author will not try and redefine project

management in this report, however here are a few things to consider:

Understand the real and practical Full Time Equivalent (FTE) resource: Project managers rarely understand what really is an FTE. An FTE is the work one person can do in one day. One day is commonly considered to be an eight hour work day. However, in practice no one works an effective full eight hours (sustainable over the long term) in one day. No matter how hard a person works, on average only about six effective hours are available in an eight hour day. Between breaks, meals, meetings, interruptions, the various crisis that pop up in every organization, vacations, sick, etc. even six hours a day is a highly effective resource.

When loading resources you should consider not work effort days (or units or other esoteric measurements), but work effort hours where six hours results in a scheduled day.

Properly load resources: Consider the common scenario in which a project manager consults with a development team on planning a project.

Expert resources will commonly double the amount of ideal work effort estimated for a task that they report to the project manager. Based on experience, resources know that nothing ever goes as planned and that padding is required to reach a true estimate.

The project manager will argue this estimate. Since the project has a fixed time line some new, agreed upon estimate will be entered into the fixed schedule.

What then commonly occurs is the resources are overloaded due to both the adjusted estimates and the inevitable cramming of the entire project into the fixed schedule.

The author has seen project managers regularly overload resources to 200% and more. Often the project manager will not even consult the project resource reports to see the overloading. They simply throw resources at a task based on resource experience rather than availability.

Project managers should listen to the expert resources and use their estimates. If the project does not fit the fixed schedule then adjustments should be made. In no case should these adjustments create a resource overload. You can just about guarantee poor project results of resources are overloaded.

Trainers

Depending on the size and complexity of your project you may need a training team to educate the users on the new system. Training and training techniques is an entire

Image courtesy of Renjith Krishnan/FreeDigitalPhotos.net

domain in many companies and there is innumerable literature on the subject. If your company is large enough to have a training team, then take advantage of their services and incorporate them early into the project. Training departments often create and support the user documentation for a system. Again, take advantage of this if possible. Training should not write system documentation. Except for the smallest organizations, developers should not be trainers. Training is generally not in the developers experience domain and once the developer is presented (as teacher) to every user, the flood of support questions inevitably follows, rendering the developer ineffective for development projects. If developers must be trainers then allot enough time and training for the developer so that their training of the users is successful. Then be sure and put the developer off limits to support questions.

Support

Except for small organizations you should have a dedicated support team. This team should be well trained (and rewarded) and be able to handle all but the most complex support incidents. You should rarely call in members of the development team on support calls. These are extremely distracting and time consuming to the development team. Too much involvement in support can bring other projects to a grinding halt.

The tools and techniques for recording support incidents is up to your organization, but it should not be so onerous as to be more effort than the actual incident support.

Management

Simply and bluntly put, management's role, like government's, should be to get out of the way of the people. Frankly management tends to micro-manage too much.

Like project management there is an entire industry supporting management theory and tools, and obviously management needs to get involved in a project and make sure that the project managers keep the project on track. However, beyond the mandated HR roles, management's main role is to remove obstacles to the project and then stay out of the way.

How Should Teams be Formed?

It is recommended that management not force team composition. On the other hand, self organizing teams are inherently risky also. As such, you must strike a balance between the two.

Management, in cooperation with the potential team members must assess the project requirements and the expertise needed to meet the requirements. When this is complete the team will have a better understanding of the potential members that can fulfill the expertise requirements. You can then complete the team.

Be sure to consider the actual availability of the potential members. A preferred member may not be available due to other commitments. Be sure to understand the resource loading of the project and other projects on which the members may be working.

In addition, be sure to consider the extended members that may be required for the project but are not part of your resource pool of team members. This is regularly overlooked but is particularly critical in today's large project environments. Often extended team members are not even discovered until well into the project development phase. At this point it is a complete surprise to the extended team member that their expertise is required.

Who Manages the Team?

As recommended, management should generally take a hands-off approach to micro-managing a project. Teams of professionals, even as artists, should be able to accomplish a certain level of self management. Good project managers will also apply a certain level of management to a project as they enforce task and milestone completion.

However, in the event that a project gets off track it is important to asses why it is off track. Do not assume that people are not working hard enough or that you should throw more resources at the project.

Projects can get off track for a multitude of reasons, but reasons that often reoccur are:

Technical difficulties
A technical issue resulting from a requirement is creating a roadblock of some type. The obvious solution is to analyze it and remove the roadblock. Be sure that the team is properly focused on the correct issue rather than simply a minor distraction issue.

Personality difficulties
Teams members will have personal conflicts that

impact projects. This is an HR related management issue and not a technical issue.

Resource availability

Proper project and resource assessment will prevent most of these issues, but when it occurs it is usually related to an extended member/resource as described in team formation. Do your best to anticipate this and work with the management of the extended resource. It may take several layers of management to solve this.

Too many tools

Your resources should not be burdened by unproductive tool sets. A key issue of this type is project progress management. In other words, the process of reporting project progress is hindering the progress. Management likes to see project metrics such as burn rate, milestones, defect rates, etc. This is useful only to management so be sure that your reporting tools do not get in the way of the project.

In addition, developers have a tendency to want to use the latest and greatest tools and to follow the advice of respected gurus in the industry. This often creates an unending learning curve of new tools resulting in overall ineffective development. Stick to a limited number of proven tools.

When a project actually is off track then management must step in. In this case the main focus is not to assess blame but to remove roadblocks, offer alternatives (brainstorming with the team often results in self-resolving alternatives) and refocus the team on the project priorities.

Dump the politics

Corporate politics (and gossip) have no business in the development process. Politics almost always result in a dispirited and unfocused team. One of a manager's key roles (related to removing road blocks) is to protect the team from politics.

This is not to say that managers should hide information from the teams or lie in favor of project progress and efficiency. Rather managers should screen, filter and clarify the politics and gossip that naturally occur in organizations. This is a tough task as managers cannot know everything said in the work environment. A better approach is to be sure that the team members are secure enough to approach management with any concerns and when politics does rear its ugly head, be proactive and address it before it festers in the team ranks.

Establish your Teams

The challenge then becomes establishing your teams!

Week Two Action Plan

Define the core resources available

That can form your immediate teams for which you have managerial control.

Define the matrix resources available

That can or will become extended resources for your teams. Be sure to include the stakeholders and subject matter experts.

Analyze your project(s) with your teams

To define all of the resources required to complete your projects.

Form your teams

And begin the deep analysis of your projects.

Week Three: Define Your Tools

Development tools are defined here as the various hardware and software items that are used to assist in developing the project infrastructure and achieving the project outcome. These include the Integrated Development Environment (IDE), Database system tools, Object Relational Management (ORM) tools, layout tools, deployment environments and techniques, etc. A list or comparison of tools is not in the scope of this report, but there are innumerable tools on the market.

In our experience it is almost universally observed that development teams try to use too many tools in their development efforts. This can lead to tool paralysis, or the inability to use all of the tools effectively. Developers will often spend too much time trying to use a wide variety of tools in the mistaken belief that more tools make better software and that tools save time (usually thinking that the tools reduce the amount of coding effort).

Tools in and of themselves are neither good nor bad. It

is the over dependence on the tools or the belief that many tools make better code that is the culprit.

As such the author recommends the following:

Define your tools

The team should settle on a core set of tools for all development. Rarely are all the team members satisfied with the sum total of the tools selected, but if decided upon as a team then team member buy-in is generally not a big problem.

Industry standard tools are recommended as there is a large body of work and support for the tool. In today's world open source products are as good and often better than the costly private label

Image courtesy of Gualberto 107/FreeDigitalPhotos.net

tools (of which many are actually based on the open source tools).

However, do not ignore the lesser known tools if they fit a specialized requirement. For example, a resource (known to the author) was tasked with developing a complex medical system requiring the use of specialized encoding process. An obscure library was just the ticket to developing the code to complete the project.

Fewer, better tools

As suggested, too many tools can lead to tool paralysis. While a thorough study of tools may turn up a better way to solve a problem, the research and learning curves, as well as the long term support needs may not be worth the value of the new tool. Look closely at the requirements to see if they can be solved with the existing tools even if it requires some more coding. For example, do you really need that full featured and complex ORM tool just to make a few database connections and data reads, or will basic data access code solve the problem and reduce your dependency on yet another complex tool.

Management tools

These include the tools used to track the project tasks, metrics and resource time. They can be simple or complex. Unless management requires some very specific metrics these types of tools should be as simple, painless and quick to use as possible. Resources spending too much time reporting to management are not actually producing.

Testing tools

The QA team will need to determine what tools best address the teams needs, but as with development, too many tools can slow things down. Good QA testing still requires a lot of hands on steps.

Be aware of the QA management tools in addition to test tools. A bug reporting or time reporting tool can be just as complex and time consuming as any other tool. If QA and the corresponding development resources are bogged down reporting and managing bug metrics rather than fixing the bugs then time is wasted.

Support

The issue of support is both a resource issue and a tools issue (and often a training issue too). Good support requires good resources (as previously described) and good tools. End users are trained in the use of the projects deployed, but cannot be expected to understand their inner workings. When they report a problem it is often a cryptic error message or simply a how-to question. Support tools can involve both the front end tools with which the end user interfaces when reporting an issue, and the back end tools with which the support resources work on issues and report support metrics.

As much as possible the support tool of choice for the end user should be a human voice with the attributes of a good resource as described throughout this report. End users that need support are quickly frustrated by online bug reporting tools, long phone menus, cryptic choices and language barriers.

The tools that support resources use should be as simple as possible so that focus is on the problem at hand and not the tool. While support metrics are important to management they should not override the fundamental need to resolve the actual support problem.

Environments and Deployments

Often overlooked in a project is the longer term deployment of the product and the tools and systems that make up the deployment environments and the deployment process.

Every project has its unique requirements and it is beyond the scope of this report to plumb the depths of things like automated testing, continuous integration and continuous deployment for which the details can be researched independently.

That being said, the author recommends:

Tiered deployment environments

Usually a development, QA and pre-production environment are sufficient for most projects. The development of high volume products may require a load testing environment, but as the best load testing should be done on an environment that truly duplicates the final production environment, the pre-production environment may be a proper choice. The QA and pre-production environments should be set up as close to the capabilities of the production environments as possible.

Separate hardware environments

Separate and isolated environments corresponding to the tiered deployment environments insure that configuration issues are well vetted.

Parallel deployment

With the advent of continuous integration and deployment the concept of a parallel deployment is often overlooked. In a parallel deployment a new release is deployed independent (and in parallel) of the existing system being upgraded by the new release. In essence, both systems can run independent of each other. Although the tiered deployment model simulates a parallel deployment to some degree, the final production deployment is where a parallel deployment can be most productive. Instead of overwriting the existing (and proven) production environment, the new release is installed, started and validated independent (in parallel) of the existing system. If the new release fails, the existing release is undamaged. If successful, the old release is simply turned off and uninstalled at a convenient time. Otherwise, in the event of a failed new release, backing out a new release and reinstalling an old release is fraught with as many potential problems as any new release to production.

Implement Your Tools

The challenge then becomes implementing your tools!

Week Three Action Plan

Review your existing tools

Determine what has really worked in the past and what has not. Toss the tools that do not add to your productivity.

Determine if any new tools (or updates to existing tools) can improve your process

Do not use this as an excuse to go play with tools. This is to determine ways to improve your process not add more tools.

Select your tools

Make the final selection and stick to it unless obvious problems show up later.

Make tool documentation available to all

Resources should not have to hunt down information that has probably already been found by someone else.

Define the tool configuration

Tools have options for setting the tool features. Define

and document a team wide set of configurations. Be flexible. Use what works for your team regardless of what some industry guru states.

Train on the final tool set

Be sure that you can make effective use of the final tool set.

Implement

Use the tools in your work. Watch for rogue tools and vet if necessary.

Week Four: Implement

All of your work comes to fruition at the point when the planning is over and it is time to implement the decisions that you have made.

This is, of course, easier said than done. Change is difficult and implementing change is even more difficult. However, if you believe that your decisions are sound, then your implementation should go smoother. More importantly, if the source members of your potential team believe that the decisions are sound then the implementation will likely proceed even smoother.

No Baby Steps... Implement It All

As much as possible all elements of your plan should be implemented. Hanging on to old ways as you implement new ways can be confusing and dispiriting. In addition the old processes will likely conflict and cause problems with the new processes.

Of course, you can only implement your changes to the limits of your management authority. As such, you will likely have conflicts with other teams that are not on the same implementation page as you are.

In the author's opinion the following steps will support your implementation:

Change is Hard

Change can be exciting and beneficial. But it is also hard. It is particularly hard on the resources that are going to implement it or those impacted by it. In addition, your changes can impact teams far beyond your immediate team.

Do not deny that change is hard. In fact, embrace the hardship to the extent that it facilitates communications within and across teams. Be ready for questions, suggestions, change requests to the changes, push back, complaints, even some subtle rebellion.

Do NOT treat the reaction to the change with the oft-heard management response of "If you don't like it you can find another job..." This is particularly insulting and dispiriting to your resources. In addition, they just may take you up on your threat and leave.

Instead, patiently listen and address the concerns as much as possible, but do not back off from your implementation. Doing so will just create implementation

paralysis as you continually try and adjust your implementation to the concerns and complaints. However, make note of all concerns and consider an *Implementation Version Two* in order to make adjustments where issues are found.

The Importance of Buy-in

Local team and extended team buy-in is critically important. Without a critical mass of buy-in you may want to rethink the implementation and step back to review your plan.

As detailed earlier, the entire process as described in this report should be a cooperative effort of your entire local team. As such, the team should have a good idea as to the changes that are to be implemented and by default provide the level of buy-in needed for a successful implementation.

Extended team buy-in is important but harder to achieve if you have no managerial control. See Communication Interfaces below.

Communicate

Communication of the plan, like buy-in, is critical and should be an on-going process of the planning.

However, in larger corporate situations communication with extended teams can be the weak link in implementation. If the plan does impact extended teams then you will likely need higher level management approval and this should facilitate communications beyond your team. Communication Interfaces, as will be described, can also help.

Develop Communication Interfaces with Extended Teams

Unless your management level is high enough to include the extended teams with which your team will be working (thus the extended teams are essentially your local teams), you will need to learn to work with the extended teams that may not implement (or have any idea of) your changes. In this situation the extended teams may have processes, protocols, documentation and management structures that are incompatible with your new process.

If not already defined in your selected development model, this situation may benefit from the concept of a team-to-team communication interface.

This may sound complicated but is essentially an agreed upon process for your team to communicate with another team. Review the Analyst description in the

Establish Your Teams section. This section also provides a good model for interfacing with extended teams (and the Analysts is a particularly good resource for this technique) such that you can define a single point for a two way input-output path and protocol between teams.

This does not have to be extremely formal, just defined and enforced. Otherwise, if all team members can communicate with all of the other extended teams (who are not implementing your plans) then you leave your team open to a plethora of communications which are more often than not uncoordinated, conflicting and confusing. This will quickly paralyze your teams effectiveness.

Expect Issues

Much like *Change is Hard* there will be issues that arise during and after your implementation. Each of these will have to be addressed on an individual bases but suffice it to say that unless you final plans are deeply flawed, do not let the issues derail your implementation.

Point Out the Rewards

Quite often the reason, value and reward of

implementing change is overlooked. Management may think that the reasons are obvious and then never really point out the reasons leaving your resources confused. Throughout the whole planning and preparation process be sure to point out why this is being implemented.

Clearly point out the personal rewards to the team members of why the changes are being implemented. These rewards should be tangible, but not material. In other words, professional resources can quickly discern the worthless value of trinkets as rewards. Feel free to handout coffee cups and pens to celebrate the implementation, but these are not rewards. Rewards are the long term and tangible benefits of the change to the work environment; the improved educational opportunities offered by the new development model; or the simpler more effective tool set, etc.

However, one material reward has both tangible and material value. This is the monetary bonus. If your budgets allow, do your best to hand out good bonuses at periodic points in time. The bonuses should be of real value (coffee house gift cards are appreciated, but of little value) and, if possible, awarded as an *after tax* amount.

Nothing is more dispiriting as receiving a sizable bonus and seeing the government (having earned none of it) take 40%-50% of the bonus. The impact to the budget is big, but the reward impact to the resource receiving the bonus is bigger.

Keep it Fun

As emphasized throughout this report software development teams are made up of artists who, in principal, generally love the work they do. However, this does not mean they love the conditions in which they work. Even a work environment that on the outside looks ideal (air-conditioned offices, good location, etc.) does not mean that the work environment is actually ideal.

While it may not be management's plan to implement changes that turn the work environment into a playground, the environment does not have to be an oppressive funeral dirge either. As much as possible encourage a pleasant and even fun work environment. Make your team want to get up in the morning and go to the office (or log into the system if they are remote). If your resources are excited about each day they go to work then they will likely produce better results as well as handle changes better.

It is a common assumption that the product is the inspiration for the enjoyment and value of the work. In the author's experience and opinion this is a false assumption. Certainly a product can be an inspiration but it is rarely the sole reason why a resource will work hard for an extended period of time. Unless the product results are significant and immediate, the inspiration of the product alone will quickly fade. The inspiration and enjoyment of the work environment is more significant.

Encourage the Craft

As reiterated throughout this report, it is the opinion of the author that the software development process should be considered a craft. It is also the author's opinion that this craft should be encouraged in your resources.

A craft is generally defined as a special skill and in our definition, one that is practiced such that the skill is improved.

Your team members are professionals. They should be treated as such and their work encouraged. This will benefit both the resources as well as you results.

Encourage the craft!

Conclusion

This Executive Report has provided the reader with the opinion of the author based on decades of experience in the field of software development.

It provides insights and advice that in the opinion of the author will help you fine tune your processes by introducing elements and ideas often overlooked in the standard professional texts and consulting services.

After reading this text it is hoped that you will be able to find new ways to enhance your teams and improve your results.